POLITICS
for
PLAIN FOLKS

James Armstrong

authorHOUSE®

AuthorHouse™
1663 Liberty Drive
Bloomington, IN 47403
www.authorhouse.com
Phone: 1 (800) 839-8640

Published by AuthorHouse 06/27/2016

ISBN: 978-1-5246-1578-9 (sc)
ISBN: 978-1-5246-1577-2 (e)

Library of Congress Control Number: 2016910200

Print information available on the last page.

Contents

Preface vii

Introduction.. ix

Chapter 1   Government: Friend Or Foe? 1

Chapter 2   Manifest Destiny:
             The Ethos Of Arrogance............................10

Chapter 3   Cuba: A Case In Point 17

Chapter 4   The Storms Of War 25

Chapter 5   Our "Cussedness" 32

Chapter 6   Our Promise 40

Chapter 7   Where Does Religion Fit In – Or Does It?.... 47

Chapter 8   Politics Where You Live 56

PREFACE

The United States is not cursed with a caste system. We have no lords and ladies representing the upper crust of our social structures, nor do we have "commoners" on a lower tier. The ground on which most of us stand is reasonably level.

Two things are undeniable.

One - local, state and national politics shape many aspects of our lives.

And two – most of you reading these words are not members of an upper class. You are not elitists; you are everyday, plain folks. You have different backgrounds. Your educations, incomes, and value systems are far from identical, but, you have far more in common than otherwise.

Politics for Plain Folks has been written for people exactly like you. I hope you find it helpful.

INTRODUCTION

If you are responsible you vote. Before casting your ballots it can be assumed that you think about any number of factors. Who is the person I am voting for? What is he or she really like? What are their values and ideals? Are the lives they live consistent with the moral standards they espouse? What are the issues at stake? How will they affect me and mine? Have I embraced a particular political school of thought? Have I given "schools of thought" any attention at all? As we think about politics for plain folks we need to begin with a belief that these matters are important.

The following pages will deal with two strands of political thought; "political realism" and "pragmatic idealism." They appear to be at opposite ends of the spectrum. Political realism seems to be hard-fisted and strong; pragmatic idealism appears to seek softer, safe, yet practical answers.

In 1945, a German American scholar named Hans Morgenthau wrote *Politics Among Nations.* He insisted that a country's foreign policy needs to be based on a willingness to use power and employ force. Later he would develop six principles of political realism.

1. Politics is governed by objective laws that have their roots in human nature.
2. Interest is defined in terms of power.
3. Power is an objective category universally valid.
4. Political action has moral significance.
5. We must not identify the moral aspirations of a particular nation with the moral laws that govern the universe.
6. The difference between political realism and other schools of thought is real.

"Interest is defined in terms of power." That sounds like a tough, two-fisted approach to public affairs – and of course, it is. Its root system goes back a long, long way.

Centuries before the dawn of the Christian era the Peloponnesian War pitted Athens against Sparta. A Greek scholar, Thucydides, thought to be the first real historian (before his time most "historians" based much of their writing on myths and legends), argued that Sparta would prevail because it was motivated by raw power rather than high-minded principles.

Centuries later a Roman philosopher, Machiavelli, argued that political expediency should be valued above morality; that craft, duplicity and deceit are justified in statecraft.

In the 1800s an Austrian statesman named Metternich insisted that politics is based on practical and material factors and not on theories and ethical objectives. He called his beliefs the *real politik*, a political theory that decades later would be embraced by a Harvard student named Henry

Kissinger who would one day become President Richard Nixon's Secretary of State and National Security Advisor.

As a graduate student at Harvard, Kissinger would write his doctoral thesis on the *real politik*. He embraced it and later, as a Harvard professor, would teach it. Applying this theory the Kissinger/Nixon team would achieve the major foreign policy accomplishment of its Administration; a measured degree of rapprochement with both the Peoples' Republic of China and the Soviet Union.

But let's go back -

Before he left office our first president, George Washington, warned against becoming entangled in foreign affairs and alliances. A century later another president, Theodore Roosevelt, turned his back on that advice and developed a bellicose foreign policy that was symbolized by the "great white fleet" of naval warships sailing around the globe. He was demonstrating the fact that we had become a world power (that word again – "power"). He demonstrated that same muscle-flexing trait, domestically, when he de-fanged Tammany Hall, took on the so-called "robber barons" of New York, and had passed his anti-trust laws.

The hard power of political realism has been employed by many U.S. presidents. Abraham Lincoln refused to let southern states secede from the Union and defeated the Confederacy in the Civil War. Theodore Roosevelt has already been mentioned. Franklin Delano Roosevelt, Theodore's distant cousin, supported Winston Churchill before we entered World War II by authorizing the Lend-Lease program, "loaning" war-making armaments to the British. Harry Truman authorized the dropping of A-bombs on Hiroshima and Nagasaki in the most devastating display of hard power the world had ever seen. And, the Paul Wolfowitz, Donald Rumsfeld, Dick Cheney band of neo-conservatives were given full sway under President George W. Bush as the U.S., with its unilateral, preemptive strike, "shocked and awed" Iraq into total submission, reducing a once noble nation into a heap of toxic rubble in what some have called the most unconscionable war in our nation's history.

We could write about the hard power employed by Alabama's county and city law enforcement officers as they confronted peaceful demonstrators trying to cross Pettis bridge in Selma in 1965, or about the elder Mayor Daley in Chicago (note the Democratic Convention in 1968). From Boston and Baltimore in the northeast to Los Angeles (Watts) in the southwest, from Seattle in the northwest to Groveland, Florida in the southeast, with a bloody pause in the Midwest's Ferguson, Missouri, violent expressions of police authority have demonstrated the harsh outer edges of political realism.

Hard power is not always violent and destructive, nor is political realism limited to the force of arms. More frequently it expresses itself in laws passed by legislative bodies or by policies adopted by town councils. Even so, it always demonstrates some of the points made by Hans Morgenthau in his "six principles."

Now – what about pragmatic idealism? "Pragmatic idealism" is a phrase first used by the American philosopher John Dewey in 1917. If political realism is symbolized by hard power, pragmatic idealism is symbolized by soft power. It is what Condoleeza Rice, our first female African-American Secretary of State, called "transformational diplomacy."

In all probability the most eloquent expression of pragmatic idealism in the history of the human family is the example of Mohandas K. (Mohatma) Gandhi in the 20th century. With his "salt march to the sea," his exemplary willingness to fast to the point of near starvation, to be beaten and bullied, to be imprisoned time and again for conscience's sake, he and his followers wrested a nation of more than 400,000,000 souls from the firm grasp of the British Empire and won its political freedom and a pathway toward democracy.

All of this, from Sparta's war against Athens in ancient Greece, to Gandhi's twisting the tail of the British lion in the 20th century, has made for some tough, demanding reading. Necessarily so. Plain people are not stupid people. We need to deal with reality; with cold, hard facts. Only then can we move on to propose hopeful pathways into the future.

The following pages will deal with the role of government in our lives; with the cultural arrogance of Manifest Destiny and with Cuba as "a case in point;" with the storms of war that have pelted humankind; with the "cussedness" and promise of human beings; e.g., with people exactly like us. They will deal with neighbors and friends, and with historic foes. They will probe the place of religion in public life.

Finally, they will come to a halt as we consider politics as practiced in the places where we live.

We began by suggesting that political realism and pragmatic idealism are at opposite ends of the spectrum. Morgenthau insisted that "the difference between political realism and other schools of thought is real." True enough. However, it will be our purpose to bring the best of these two worlds, political realism and pragmatic idealism, together. If we can do that we will have developed an approach to politics for plain folks that will benefit both ourselves and future generations.

GOVERNMENT: FRIEND OR FOE?

Is government our friend or our foe? Does that sound like a silly question? Not if you consider the number of people who consider government an enemy.

From Libertarians and Tea Party advocates on the right to Noam Chomsky and anarchists on the left, there are those who feel that government, more often than not, is opposed to the common good.

The so-called Tea Party has exercised undue influence on the politics of our time. Jim Wallis, the brilliant editor of *Sojourners,* has written about the "theology" of the Tea Party. He says the Tea Party believes that –

- individual rights are all important;
- let private charity take care of the least among us;
- we should claim human rights for ourselves;
- government is the enemy;
- the free market will take care of itself; and,
- the "spoils" belong to the strong.

Ayn Rand, a refugee who came to the United States from Russia after the Bolshevist revolution, developed a school of thought she called "objectivism." She considered the State, any state, an enemy. A generation of college students was fascinated by her. She looked like a Russian countess and was persuasive and, in her own way, charismatic. She disliked men and used and treated them much as macho men are said to treat women. She likened government, any government, to the Soviet Union she had left behind. According to her, governing bodies stood in the way of individual freedom.

Ronald Reagan once famously said that "Government is not a solution to our problems, government *is* our problem," and Reagan has become the patron saint of the Republican party. For the past twenty-five years many right-wing politicos have insisted that government is dysfunctional, corrupt, intrusive, exploitive, bloated and sinfully deceptive, and under them it has been: dysfunctional (as in Homeland Security, Katrina, and "no exit strategy" from Iraq); corrupt (as in Halliburton, Blackwater and Jack Abramoff); intrusive (as in wire-tapping, the Patriot Act, and lurking in our bedrooms); exploitive (as in blatant fear-mongering following 9/11); bloated (as in a national debt amounting to trillions of dollars); and sinfully deceptive (as in Guantanimo, enhanced interrogation techniques, and the neo-con madness that thrust us into Iraq). Government can be the enemy of our common good. It should not be.

Government is defined as "the administration of public policy." Is public policy desirable? Of course it is. Is its administration necessary? Of course it is.

Jonathan Alter, in his book, *The Defining Moment*, described Franklin D. Roosevelt's first one hundred days in office. He argued that FDR saved our democracy, spared our land from a violent blood-letting, and restored hope to a people ravaged by unemployment, hunger and homelessness; the by-products of the Great Depression.

In his Second Inaugural Address, Roosevelt took stock of his first administration. He said, "We refused to leave the problems of our common welfare to be solved by the winds of chance and the hurricanes of disaster." A remarkable leader, F.D.R. used his office and the instruments of government as tools to restore hope and breathe new life into the lungs of the American people.

How did he do it?

In 1933, during the first formative days of Roosevelt's administration, there was the alphabet soup of the New Deal: the W.P.A, (the Works Progress Administration that provided jobs for the unemployed); the P.W.A. (the Public Works Administration that did the same); the T.V.A. (the Tennessee Valley Authority that provided power, for the first time, to remote areas of our southland); the A.A.A. (the Agricultural Administration Act); the N.R.A. (the National Recovery Act); and, perhaps the most remarkable of all, the C.C.C. (the Civilian Conservation Corps).

Remember, the old guy writing these words has been around for a long, long time. His father, a reserve Army officer, was the district director of educational and religious programs for the C.C.C. in the upper peninsula of Michigan in the early 1930s. As a boy I traveled with him as he did his work. Each night, before we went to bed, we played cribbage (that's the kind of thing plain folks do, and those memories are among the warmest of my early years). I traveled with him from Camp Strong to Camp Pine River to Camp Marquette, and to other dots on Michigan's map.

I spent one summer in Camp Pine River learning to shoot pool, play table tennis, and picking up language patterns that served me well in the U.S. Navy. However, as important as anything else I learned, is what I saw. I saw young Americans swept in off the streets of Chicago and Detroit and Cincinnati and Milwaukee, planting trees, and building dams and roads, as they worked to reclaim and conserve the natural environment of our land.

As Alter reminded his readers - over nine years more than three million men planted three billion trees, developed eight hundred state parks, protected twenty million acres of land from erosion, and cleared 125,000 miles of trails. Not only that, but the C.C.C. inspired hosts of later programs – the Peace Corps, the Job Corps, VISTA, Americorps, and thousands of community projects.

Jonathan Alter wrote, "Roosevelt's point was plain: government counts. And in the right hands it can be made to work. Strong federal action, not just private voluntary efforts and the invisible hand of the market place, was required...

The American people expected and deserved leadership in addressing their hardships, not just from state and local authorities, but from the White House. This fundamental insight would guide politicians and help millions of people in the years ahead." It was government – *government* – that made all of this possible!

Government can be a friend – or, as has been suggested, it can be a foe: as in Hitler's Germany; in Stalin's Soviet Union; in Franco's Spain; in Mussolini's Italy; and, in Governor Rick Snyder's Flint, Michigan.

Rachel Maddow's remarkable investigative journalism and President Obama's visit to the city brought Flint's story to the attention of the American people. Outside experts were saying that there was a problem with Flint's water system. Flint's water had come from Detroit, but in order to save money the governor and his state-appointed city manager switched from Detroit's system to the Flint River. Alarmingly, tests showed that old pipes had corroded allowing lead to leak into Flint's water system. The lead content of the water was poisoning Flint's people. Authorities said that it could cause brain damage to little children.

In September of 2015 Governor Snyder insisted there was no problem. He was contradicted by the Michigan Department of Environmental Quality and the state's Department of Health and Human Services. Meaningful conversations and apologies followed, but the damage had been done.

Legionairres disease, linked to Flint's water problem, claimed ten people's lives and affected another 77 people.

The outspoken movie producer, Michael Moore, a native of Flint, called for Governor Snyder's arrest. That was not likely to happen. But Snyder's fellow-Republican, Ted Cruz, a presidential candidate at the time, said, "It is a failure of officials, state officials, and the men and women of Flint have been betrayed,"

On April 26, 2016, criminal charges for misconduct in office were filed against city officials Michael Prysby and Stephen Busch. Former city water plant operator Michael Glasgow was charged with filing false information. In Flint, Michigan, government had become a criminal.

Once again – government can be a gracious friend. It can also be a formidable foe. It need not be.

Many right-wing politicians argue that government has no business involving itself in the every-day lives of people. They need to be reminded that a Republican president, Abraham Lincoln, developed a national railway system; that a Republican president, Theodore Roosevelt, had anti-trust and anti-monopoly laws passed; that a Republican president, Dwight D. Eisenhower, was responsible for developing our national highway system. Assuming responsibility for the American people's "general welfare" is a bi-partisan enterprise.

American presidents deliver annual State of the Union messages. Think of what some of our presidents from both parties have said about public concerns and responsibilities in their annual messages:

Franklin Delano Roosevelt in 1935: 'In spite of our efforts and in spite of our talk we have not weeded out the overprivileged and we have not effectively lifted up the underprivileged."

Harry Truman in 1948: "It is deplorable that for a nation as rich as ours there are millions of children who do not have adequate schoolhouses or enough teachers for a good elementary or secondary education."

Dwight D. Eisenhower in 1953: "There is urgent need for greater effectiveness in our programs, both public and private, offering safeguards against the privations that too often come with unemployment, old age, illness and accident."

Ronald Reagan in 1984: "We know that many of our countrymen are still out of work, wondering what will come of their hopes and dreams. Can we love America and not reach out to tell them: You are not forgotten; we will not rest until each of you can reach out as high as your God-given talents can take you."

Two Republican and two Democrat "governors;" that is, persons who governed - expressing ideals that captured the hope and promise of our republic. How can government come to grips with challenges like these? Their idealism needed to be joined by political realism.

Government exists at virtually every level of our existence. There are governing bodies at regional, state and local levels,

At the regional level there have been organizations like the Southern Poverty Law Center (the SPLC) and the Southern Christian Leadership Conference (SCLC) that may not govern, but they represent values and they influence public policy. The SPLC has spent endless hours testifying at Congressional hearings, and has filed a flood of suits on behalf of its underprivileged clients.

Some years ago the South Carolina Christian Knights of the Ku Klux Klan burned down a historic black church. The SPLC sued the KKK and won the suit. The result was a $37.8 million verdict against the KKK, "the biggest-ever civil award for damages in a hate crime" according to the *Washington Post.* It broke the back of South Carolina's KKK, putting it out of business forever.

Regional bodies may not govern, but they can surely impact public affairs.

State governments determine minimum wages, tax policies related to corporate entities and individuals, safety standards for workplaces, and a host of other matters related to the public's well-being.

Sometimes state governments are the problem.

Following the Plessy-Ferguson Supreme Court (separate-but-equal) decision in the 1890s, southern states passed and enforced laws related to racial segregation that dehumanized large segments of America's population.

Currently some states have passed discriminatory laws victimizing members of the GLBT (Gay, Lesbian, Bisexual, Transexual) community, singling out the transgendered for special humiliating reprisal.

We are fortunate that the Constitution with its Bill of Rights, and federal laws, are binding upon states. "States rights" cannot successfully defy federal legislation.

Local governments (a later chapter will deal with local governments in detail) determine things like speed limits, parking zones, bicycle paths, rest room uses, and public recreation areas, etc.

We would be left tossed about in a sea of confused contradictions and warring factions, without government.

In spite of the Ayn Rands of this world, governing bodies are here to stay. They are essential organisms in a well-ordered society. It is up to people like you and me, the plain folks these words are addressed to, to give shape and direction to the ideals and aspirations of the most thoughtful among us.

MANIFEST DESTINY:
THE ETHOS OF ARROGANCE

In 1630 John Winthrop, one of our Pilgrim forefathers, preached a famous sermon. Speaking of the American colonies he said, "We must consider that we shall be a city on a hill. The eyes of all people will be upon us."

Tom Paine, in his revolutionary tract *Common Sense,* wrote, "We have within our power to begin the world over again."

Herman Melville, the author of *Moby Dick,* wrote. "We Americans are the peculiar, chosen people – the Israel of our time – the political messiah has come in us."

During the Spanish American War, Indiana's Senator Beveridge wrote, "God has marked the American people to finally lead to the redemption of the world. This is the divine mission of America."

President Woodrow Wilson put it more bluntly: "America has the infinite privilege of fulfilling her destiny and saving the world."

Those exaggerated self-impressions were not limited to Americans. Early in the 19th century the French political philosopher and world traveler, Alexis de Tocqueville, came to our shores. Writing from a European's vantage point he cited our multi-ethnic amalgam of immigrants as a key to our unique identity and destiny. He wrote, "Everything about America is extraordinary."

De Tocqueville spoke of our natural boundaries and resources. We had coastlines facing two oceans; raw materials beyond belief; arable farm lands; some of the world's richest fishing areas; and, two-thirds of our vast land was inhabitable. De Tocqueville added this distinctive word:

"Physical causes contribute less (to America's distinctiveness) than laws and mores."

In 1845, the newspaper editor, John O'Sullivan, coined the term, "manifest destiny." To embrace the phrase is to embrace the idea that we have special "laws and mores" (values and virtues) and an ordained mission under divine Providence; "we," in this case, meaning people like many of us reading these words – WASPs (White Anglo-Saxon Protestants). Others were considered lesser breeds. That, good reader, was an "ethos of arrogance."

The so-called Monroe Doctrine, written by John Adams in 1823, is not unrelated to Manifest Destiny. The Monroe Doctrine insisted that Europe would no longer be permitted to colonize or interfere in the affairs of the independent nations of the Americas. Adams opposed colonization of any sort. That ship sailed when President Theodore Roosevelt led us into the Spanish-American War and we "acquired" the Philippines, Guam and Hawaii. We had become an "empire." The Caribbean Sea had become "an American lake." What followed?

- We invaded Cuba in 1898 and occupied it from 1906 to 1912;
- for thirty years Cuba was required to submit proposed laws to the U.S. Congress for approval;
- we colonized Puerto Rico in 1898;
- we occupied the Dominican Republic in 1910;
- we occupied Nicaragua from 1912 to 1933;
- we aided in the overthrow of Guatemala's elected government in 1954;
- we aided in the overthrow of the Brazilian government in 1954;
- we organized the invasion of Cuba's Bay of Pigs in 1961;
- we invaded Haiti in 1965 and occupied it for more than thirty years;
- our CIA joined with the ITT (International Telephone and Telegraph Company) to overthrow Salvador Allende's freely elected, constitutional socialist Chilean government in 1973, only to replace it with Pinochet's reign of violent military tyranny;
- we armed and supported the Contras as they fought the Sandonistas in Central America beginning in 1979 (this was justified as "necessary" because the Cold War pitted us against the Soviet Union and

the Sandonistas were thought to tilt toward the Soviets);

- Reagan invaded the Falkland Islands and Granada; to boost our morale and help us get over the checkmate in Vietnam we were told. One critic suggested it was like an elephant stomping on an ant;

- we invaded Haiti again in 1994; and,

- following Kuwait, the Bush administration "shocked and awed" Iraq into submission, foolishly believing we could impose Jeffersonian democracy on Iraq and Middle Eastern nations in spite of the fact that they were self-proclaimed theocracies bound by the Koran, Sunni and Shia loyalties, Saudi law, and Wahabi teaching.

Was this what destiny manifested? *"The ethos of arrogance!"*

Manifest Destiny, with its WASP mentality, victimized multitudes of people. Notable among them was the Native American. We violated or nullified any number of treaties with American Indians. A typical example: we had ceded the Black Hills of South Dakota to Native Americans. Gold was discovered in the hills. We promptly cancelled that treaty agreement and exchanged the Black Hills for a barren valley to be called the Pine Ridge Indian Reservation.

AIM (the American Indian Movement), headed by two Indians from Cleveland, Russell Means and Dennis Banks, led a group of Native American activists on what they called "the trail of tears." They revisited sites that had been taken from them by the U.S. government. From Oklahoma they ventured north, until they arrived, at long last, at the Pine River Reservation in South Dakota. They took hostages and for seventy-one days in early 1973 they occupied Wounded Knee, a town on the Pine Ridge Reservation and the site of the last massacre of the Indian wars of the nineteenth century.

Armed federal marshals were brought in to quell the revolt. Your author, who was stationed in South Dakota at the time, was asked by the National Council of Churches to help resolve the crisis. It was an eerie experience to enter the besieged Reservation, driving by armed Federal marshals at one check point and passing armed Native Americans at a later check point. Your author has in his possession a prized *Rocky Mountain News* photo, with the caption, "Two Indians wounded; talks resumed." It shows Russell Means and Dennis Banks clasping hands with "the Rt. Rev. James Armstrong, United Methodist bishop for North and South Dakota agreeing to a cease fire."

When the occupation ended, Elliot Richardson, the Assistant Attorney General of the U.S., summoned a few of us to Washington, D.C., to thank us for helping avert widespread bloodshed.

So much for one of the harsh by-products of Manifest Destiny!

Manifest Destiny is not unrelated to a belief in American "exceptionalism." Most sovereign nations believe they are exceptional. That is understandable and is as it should be, unless it leads to an Adolf Hitler's insane belief in an Aryan

German "master race," or a Benito Mussolini's black shirt brand of Fascism, or our own "America First" mania of the 1930s.

In 1787, Alexander Hamilton wrote, "It seems to have been reserved to the people of this country, by their conduct and example, to decide the important question, whether societies of men are capable of establishing good government from reflection and choice, or whether they are forever destined to depend for their political constitution on accident and force."

While applauding the Tony-award winning Broadway play, "Hamilton," we need to acknowledge that Alexander Hamilton had little sympathy for the "lower classes" in his own country.

Most Americans believe that we are an exceptional nation. As indicated earlier, de Tocqueville outlined many of the reasons why we are an exceptional land. You can develop your own list of values and virtues. However, we need to be reminded that everything was not sunshine and roses. We are the only western democracy that practiced slavery well into the industrial age. We have the highest crime rate and the highest rate of imprisonment among industrialized nations. Gun violence is a national scandal. And, we spend more on "defense" than the next eight nations combined – and many of them are our allies.

Manifest Destiny is said to relate to our professed values, our sense of mission, and our belief that all of this is "under God." But, think for a moment. Our values are spelled out in our Constitution with its Bill of Rights, and our Declaration of Independence. Our mission needs to be a blend of humanitarian servitude (not triumphalism - might does not make right) and international strength based on political realism blended with pragmatic idealism.

Manifest Destiny is not the answer. Its ethos of arrogance poses a major problem. We are not called upon to strut pompously into the future, but rather to love righteousness and mercy, to embrace justice, and to walk humbly with our God.

CUBA: A CASE IN POINT

Cuba was one of the victims of the Monroe Doctrine and Manifest Destiny. At the end of the Spanish American War we took Cuba as our own possession. The Platt Amendment, adopted by our Congress in 1901, listed seven conditions that should be met before the United States would agree to withdraw its troops. In the meantime the President of the U.S. would function as Cuba's Provisional Governor. Cuban laws would have to be approved by the U.S. Congress. It was all detailed, and we were the "conquering heroes."

Before dealing with more recent times, let's go back.

Jose Marti, born in 1853, a poet (he wrote the lyrics for Cuba's most well known patriotic song, "Guantanimero") and political activist, was both the spiritual and literal father of Cuba's independence. When only 16 years of age he was imprisoned by the Spaniards for his anti-government activities (he had scars on his wrists and ankles, from the chains that bound him, for the rest of his life). He was exiled to Spain where he studied law. He returned to Cuba and then moved to New York City where he guided the direction of Cuba's war for independence. He feared for

Cuba's domination by either Spain or the United States. In 1895, he returned to the battlefield in Cuba and was killed in action. Cuban consulates and Cuban restaurants across our land feature pictures of Jose Marti (we have one taken in a local bistro).

Now move forward to the infamous role of Fulgencio Batista. He led a military coup in 1952, and, backed by the U.S. government, he presided over what President John F. Kennedy called, "one of the most bloody and reprehensible dictatorships of Latin American repression."

Move the clock forward again. On January 1, 1959, Fidel Castro and Che Guevera, after long months of guerilla warfare in the Sierra Maestro Mountains, came down into Havana and Santiago and seized the reins of government. Batista had reported Castro's death "during the July 26 landing." Batista was wrong. Obviously, Castro was very much alive.

Batista's Cuba had become known as the "whorehouse of the Caribbean." Corrupt to the core, Batista had ties with the Mafia, and was linked to prostitution, gambling, and a host of other underworld activities.

When Castro's victory was imminent Batista fled the island with many of his comrades-in-arms, and with some $300 million he had criminally amassed. As an exile he fled to dictator Trujillo's Dominican Republic. From there he proceeded to Portugal. He died in Spain of a heart attack in 1973.

Your author was serving a church in Indianapolis in 1959. The church sponsored missionaries in Santiago de las Vegas, a suburb of Havana. We had built an educational building adjacent to the church. In January, three weeks after Castro came to power, I flew into Havana to dedicate the building. What I saw was beyond belief.

I wrote my mother a letter (remember, this was 1959), and said: "I am appalled by the manner in which American congressmen and newspapers have interpreted these events. The people are delirious with a new hope for 'libertad.' My first full day here was Jose Marti Day. Marti is Cuba's Washington. He was killed in the war for independence in 1895, after engineering it from New York City. For the first time in seven years the people were able to have patriotic parades. I attended one. When a truckload of 'barbudos' (bearded ones) passed by the children clapped and their elders cheered.

"We hear about the execution of 400 persons (and there have been unfortunate, but perhaps understandable, reprisals), but, have we heard of the slaughter of 20,000 by Batista, his armies and his police? With others I visited the Santa Clara Police Station and saw instruments of torture designed to remove finger nails, break bones, take eyes out, and send electric currents into the ears and genitals. Ventura, Batista's henchman, was in charge.

"The Cuban air force bombed Cienfuegos in 1957 and Santa Clara in 1958, as Cubans killed fellow Cubans. Now the lid has blown off and I'm amazed by the restraint of the new government.

"Yesterday we drove down to our seminary in Matanzas. I spoke in the chapel and had my picture taken with a group of dirty, bewhiskered barbudos, guns in hand and all. They seem to be a happy lot of country boys who have come to the big city to build a new nation. Last night one came into the church service where I was speaking, plopped down on the pew holding his machine gun aloft, and took it all in."

As indicated, I was there to dedicate a new building. The deed was done. A few months later the building was "nationalized" and converted into a school by the Castro government. Castro took over hundreds of buildings like that and they were integrated into the nation's school system. Obviously our "gift" was not voluntary, but we did contribute to the fact that Cuba has the highest literacy rate of any Latin American country.

In April of 1959, Fidel came to the United States. He visited New York City and is said to have "answered impertinent questions calmly, never lost his temper, always kept his good humor, visited the zoo, ate hot dogs and hamburgers, kissed the ladies 'like a rock star,' and staged a public relations coup".

He continued on to our nation's capitol where Eisenhower snubbed him, choosing to play golf instead of meeting with him. Vice President Nixon met with Castro for 2½ hours, considered him "terribly naïve about communism" and dangerous. He shared his negative opinions with the president. It was obvious that Castro wanted to win the favor of our national leaders. Sadly, Nixon's negative opinions prevailed.

In October 1960, President Eisenhower cancelled 700,000 tons of sugar exports and refused to export oil to Cuba. In response Cuba nationalized the American oil refineries without compensation. Cuba became reliant on Soviet crude oil and became increasingly reliant on Soviet aid.

We imposed an embargo on Cuba (Cuba called it a blockade); an embargo that lasted nearly sixty years. The United Nations condemned it. Our allies as trading partners ignored it. But the embargo prevailed.

What was life like in the Cuba of those days?

In 1977, your author, joined by Robert McAfee Brown, a noted interpreter of what was called "liberation theology," Davie Napier of the Pacific School of Religion, Alan McCoy, a Franciscan priest and president of the Conference of Major Superiors, and Russell Dilley, my administrative assistant and a former missionary to Cuba, flew down to the island nation.

We visited day care centers, schools that were based on Jose Marti's work-study ethic (three hours in the classroom and three hours working in fields or shops); an experimental dairy farm near Havana; Alamar, a model "workers' city;" and the famed Havana Psychiatric Hospital.

We met with a CDR (Committee for the Defense of the Revolution) block group and heard neighbors discuss their children's health and school problems, a woman's recent cancer diagnosis, and plans for an upcoming national festival of some sort (it was much like support groups many schools and churches have in the United States). Eighty percent of Cuba's population over 14 years of age were said to be members of CDR units.

We met with both Protestant and Roman Catholic leaders. At that time Communist Party members were not allowed to join churches and church members were not permitted to join the Communist Party. The Cuban Constitution defined Cuba as an "atheist" nation. In 1991, that was changed from atheist to "secular" and Christmas was made a national holiday.

The most significant event of our stay was a two-and-a-half-hour conversation with Fidel Castro. It was initially scheduled for twenty minutes, but "el presidente" did like the sound of his own voice. He spoke glowingly of the revolution and its place in history. His reign had already spanned the terms of several U.S. presidents and he shared his impressions.

Eisenhower, he said, was "indolent and wanted no change." Nixon was "false...he could not be trusted." LBJ "was a politician rather than a man of high principle." Castro spoke warmly of John F. Kennedy: "he matured in office... and had he lived he would have changed the character of the presidency." He called Jimmy Carter "a man of moral character" and argued that while Gerald Ford "used" Miami Cubans and intensified hostilities, "Carter refused to do that." It needs to be remembered that after 44 years Castro had outlasted ten U.S. presidents, and his analyses of our presidents, according to many pundits, were not that far off target,

When asked about political prisoners, he said there were none; only "enemies of the Revolution." According to the Independent Cuban Commission on Human Rights by January of 2002 that number had fallen from several thousand to 210.

The embargo lasted for more than half a century. Designed to either bring down the Castro government or to bring about significant change in Cuba, it did neither.

Early in 2016, President Barack Obama met with Raul Castro, Cuba's acting head-of-state. At the Summit of Americas in Panama City they talked for an hour. The ice was broken. In an agreement brokered by Pope Francis I, Obama took Cuba off the state-sponsored terror list and liberalized travel and trade restrictions. Will a GOP Congress lift the trade embargo? That remains to be seen.

Republican reactions to the new reality were sharp. Jeb Bush said, "Secretary of State John Kerry's visit to Havana…is a symbol of the Obama administration's acquiescence to Castro's ruthless legacy." Marco Rubio said, "The deal with Cuba threatens America's moral standing in our hemisphere and around the world." Ted Cruz said, "This president has shown he is willing to do what nine previous presidents of both political parties would not do – cave in to a communist dictator in our own hemisphere." Somewhat surprisingly, Donald Trump shrugged and said: "The concept of opening with Cuba is fine."

Under Obama's leadership we have turned the page. Cuba is no longer considered a member of an earlier administration's "axis of evil." Wretchedly poor and suffering under the weight of a heavy-handed bureaucracy, it is experiencing some reforms under Raul Castro, Fidel's younger brother. It poses no threat to its neighbors. It is simply a desperately poor country struggling, however imperfectly, to take its place among the family of nations.

As suggested earlier, Cuba was a victim of Manifest Destiny and the Monroe Doctrine – *the ethos of arrogance.* As relations are normalized we will be able to resume important economic and business ties, leave travel restrictions behind, and share a far more promising future.

THE STORMS OF WAR

Anohni was singing her song, "Hopelessness." Singing tenderly, as if to a lover, she sang about all kinds of organized brutality and systemic damage around the world: of public executions and torture, surveillance, ecological destruction, and technological warfare. In "Drone Bomb Me" she sang, "Blow my head off/Explode my crystal guts/Lay my purple on the grass." She sang, "If I killed your father/With a drone bomb/How would you feel?" Continuing with heart-rending empathy she concluded with the phrase, repeated over and over again, "I'm sorry/I'm sorry/I'm sorry."

Facing the reality of toxic violence and technological warfare, being sorry is not enough.

Noam Chomsky has reminded us, rightly or wrongly, that the United States has been mankind's most notable perpetrator of violent destruction. Think of our wars:

- In 1755, we fought with the British against the French and the Indians;
- in 1776 we fought our revolution, defeated the Brits, and gained our independence;

- in 1799 we fought our sea battles with the French;
- in 1812 we waged that war as the British burned our nation's capitol to the ground;
- in 1845 we defeated Mexico and the Alamo became a national symbol of heroic martyrdom (a youthful one-term Congressman from Illinois named Abraham Lincoln opposed that war);
- in the 1860s we fought the Civil War as our land was torn apart;
- in 1898 we were led up San Juan Hill by Teddy Roosevelt and were goaded into the Spanish-American War (we became an "empire" adding the Philippines, Guam, Hawaii and Puerto Rico to our turf – and the Caribbean Sea became "an American lake");
- in 1917 we entered World War I;
- the 1940s brought us into the ravages of World War II;
- in 1950 there was the Korean War;
- through the '60s and into the '70s there was Vietnam;
- in the '80s there were Granada, the Falkland islands and Panama;
- in 1999 we joined NATO as our Air Force was deployed and we sought to end "ethnic cleansing" in the Slavic states;
- then came 9/11, Afghanistan and Iraq; and,
- today there are AlQaeda, jihadists and ISIS, the State of Islam.

The above adds up to a bunch of wars. Were we always right?

What makes a war "justifiable?" Just War (morally defensible) theories have abounded since the Greeks and Romans developed them. Among others, St. Augustine tried to define a "just" war. Most theories have been boiled down to six basic principles:

1. A just war can be waged only as a last resort.
2. A war is just only if it is waged by legitimate authority.
3. A war can be fought only to redress a wrong suffered; e.g., self-defense against an armed attack.
4. A war can only be just if it is fought with a reasonable chance of success.
5. The ultimate goal of a just war is to reestablish peace.
6. The violence used in a war must be proportional to the injury suffered.

Having listed the wars the United States has been engaged in, how have we measured up? Have any of our wars been "unjust?" (Try on the Mexican War and Vietnam for size.)

In 2003, Robert McNamara's, "The Fog of War," won the Academy Award as the year's best Documentary film. McNamara stood center stage in its production as it depicted the violent brutality of World War II and the Vietnam War. It should be remembered that McNamara, our Defense Secretary at the time, was considered the architect of our involvement in Vietnam. The film also explored the implications and outcome of the Cuban Missile Crisis. Among other persons, the camera focused on General Curtis LeMay, a war criminal if ever there was one. He directed the dropping of the A-bombs on Hiroshima and Nagasaki. He believed in the total destruction of "the enemy," however we chose to define that enemy (and LeMay was "ours").

In "The Fog of War" McNamara listed eleven lessons he had learned:

1. Empathize with the enemy; that is, understand him, to the degree that is possible, from within his own psyche. (Looking at the Middle East, what did we really know about the Sunni, Shia and Kurd cultures or their history? Before that, what did we really know about the Vietnamese and their thousand year conflict with China?)
2. Rationality will not save you. (Richard Nixon and Jimmie Carter had higher IQs than Franklin Roosevelt and Ronald Reagan. Who were the more consequential? Brains alone are not enough.)
3. There is something beyond the self. (It was Martin Luther King who said we should ask ourselves each day, "What are you doing for others?" Most of the world's religions have the equivalent of the New Testament's Golden Rule).
4. Maximize efficiency. (The film featured the countless lives savedby Ford's introduction of seat belts. As McNamara reminded his viewers, he was Ford's CEO at the time).

5. Proportionality should be a guideline (today's war-making technology makes this one obsolete).

6. Get the data. (Today's political campaigns, featuring the flaws and failings of competing candidates and their spouses, with opponents looking everywhere for dirty laundry, indicate how foes exploit this one – a good but depressing example.)

7. Believing and seeing are often wrong. (As in the Bay of Tonkin resolution and the manner in which WMDs [Weapons of Mass Destruction] were used as a rationale for reducing Iraq to bloody ashes).

8. Be prepared to reexamine your own reasoning. (Compare George W. Bush's inability to think of a single wrong policy decision he had made during an early press conference to Barack Obama's frank admission, at another press conference many years later as he confessed: "I screwed up.")

9. In order to do good you may have to do harm. (former Secretary of State Madeline Albright's callous comments about "collateral damage" when referring to the women and children killed by U.S. bombs in Iraq – a case in point. But, was that "good?")

10. Never say never.

11. You can't change human nature. (We will discuss man's "cussedness" and "promise" in following chapters.)

In 1983, as president of the National Council of Churches, your author was in the Soviet Union to meet with the Patriarch of the Russian Orthodox Church. Late one night he walked through the vast expanses of the Piskarioskoye Memorial Cemetery in Leningrad (now St. Petersburg). During World War II, the city had been under siege for 900 days. More than 500,000 people had starved or were frozen to death. They had been buried in 186 mass graves in this cemetery. The somber strains of Shostokovich's 7th symphony (the composer's tribute to the victims of the siege) drifted through the night air. A huge statue of Mother Russia, in the form of a grieving mother with outstretched arms, dominated the scene. As he stood there in the darkness, listening to the somber music with his head bowed – your author wept.

Wars have been a part of the human story since the beginning of time. Theories and lessons seem to have been lost on most of us – but, thankfully, not on all of us.

The antitheses of violence are empathy and compassion. Some time ago Karen Armstrong (no relative), the uniquely gifted British thinker and writer, formed a "council of sages." The council developed a Principle of Compassion.

"The principle of compassion," they wrote, "lies at the heart of all religious groups, ethical and spiritual traditions, calling us always to treat others as we wish to be treated ourselves. Compassion impels us to work tirelessly to alleviate the suffering of our fellow creatures, to dethrone ourselves from the centre of our world and put another there, and to honor the inviolable sanctity of every human being, treating everybody, without exception, with absolute justice, equity and respect."

Understand this: you and I – each one of us – is under a mandate to do his and her part in making this a better and more wholesome world community.

Rachel Maddow, in her provocative book, *Drift: the Unmooring of American Military Power*, wrote, "Republicans and Democrats alike have options to vote people into Congress who are determined to assert the legislature's constitutional prerogatives on war and peace. It would make a difference and help reel us back toward balance and normalcy."

She closes with these words: "None of this is impossible. This isn't bigger than us. Decisions about national security are ours to make. And the good news is that this isn't rocket science (remember – this book is designed to reach into the minds of everyday people; of plain folks) – we don't need to reinvent…We just need to revive that old idea of America as a deliberately peaceable nation. That's not simply our inheritance, it's our responsibility."

OUR "CUSSEDNESS"

Few things illustrate the "sinfulness" of the human species more fatalistically than the curse of war. As suggested in the last chapter, it seems to be in our DNA.

Hans Morgenthau suggested that "politics is governed by objective laws that have their roots in human nature."

Another important political realist in twentieth century America was Reinhold Niebuhr. There were five recurring themes in his thought:

1. An explicit nature of man;
2. a distrust of moral perfectability;
3. the importance of history;
4. avoidance of moral absolutes; and,
5. the inescapable role of power politics.

A starting point for both Niebuhr and Morgenthau was human nature, and both men took a dim view of human nature. It is said that Niebuhr rediscovered the biblical notion of "original sin."

Many of the plain folks reading these words grew up in religious households. You remember the words of the gospel songs you heard or sang:

> "What a friend we have in Jesus, all our sins and griefs to bear."

> "I was sinking deep in sin, far from the peaceful shore."

> "There is a fountain filled with blood, drawn from Emmanuel's veins and sinners plunged beneath that flood……"

> "Change and decay in all around I see…"

Sin and decay were recurring themes.

It was Jonathan Edwards, the famed pre-Revolutionary Congregational pastor, who preached a sermon that typified his 18th century moment: "Sinners in the Hands of an Angry God." Sin was real, and God was the God of the Old Testament; a "dirty-bully God," according to G. Bromley Oxnam, a Methodist bishop.

The Roman Catholic Church, with its Confessional, was no better. In one of the classes your author taught at Rollins College in central Florida, we dealt with "the God-question and self-understanding." Many of our class discussions probed the depths. Several of the students who had grown up in Catholic homes told of the mental and emotional scars left as they had been required, in the Confessional, to divulge dark secrets related to their "sins."

One mother told of preparing her eight-year old son for the Confessional: he could talk about taking the Lord's name in vain, or bringing dirty, mud-soaked shoes onto a clean living room carpet; of cheating in school, or teasing his little sister. They had to manufacture something.

The Bible seems to provide little help. From the creation story in Genesis, insisting that "in Adam's fall we've sinned all;" through the Ten Commandments and the 51st Psalm; to the apostle Paul's list of every conceivable sin, real or imagined, in his letter to the Roman church; to the book of Revelation in which a sinful world endures its last days only to be swallowed up by an eternal Beyond – from the story of Adam and Eve to the predicted Apocolypse, there was little hope or promise.

Thomas Aquinas, in the 13th century, categorized seven deadly sins: avarice, envy, gluttony, lust, pride, sloth and wrath. To this day Roman Catholicism still recognizes these "deadly sins."

Sigmund Freud in his *Civilization and Its Discontents*, wrote, "The different religions have never overlooked the part played by the sense of guilt. They come forward with a claim…to save mankind from this sense of guilt, which they call sin." We need to remember that Freud, while critiquing religion, did his part in underscoring the negative underside of human nature, with his attempts to explore and define the "ego", the "id" and the "libido."

Freud didn't think much of folks like us. He once wrote. "I have found little that is 'good' about human beings on the whole. In my experience most of them are trash, no matter whether they publicly subscribe to this or that ethical doctrine." "Trash" he called us.

We don't need to rehash the theories of others. Look at your daily newspaper – or look at mine. Today, in a medium sized city, our paper contained the following:

- "Off-duty reserve officer to suspect: 'I'll blow your brains out'"

- "Report: Robbery suspect shot partner in carjacking attempt"

- "Two shot outside strip club"

- "Officer shoots unarmed black youth"

- "Ferguson seeks new tax to cover shooting cost"

- "Zimmerman gun sale stirs up debate" (Yep, *that* Zimmerman).

This is the same city where, in June of 2016, a self-radicalized ISIS believer named Omar Mateen, gunned down and killed forty-nine people, wounding another 53, in a gay-oriented night club. It was said to be the largest mass killing of its kind in our country's history.

Gun violence, aided and abetted by the NRA (National Rifle Association) and its 2nd-amendment gun-toting adherents, has become a shameful national scandal.

Don't think for a moment that "cussedness" is reserved for the disadvantaged alone. Fault and frailty plague not only the down-and-out. They plague the up-and-in as well.

Eleanor Roosevelt proved to be the social conscience of her husband, Franklin D. Roosevelt. However it was Lucy Mercer, his close companion for long years, who was with him in Warm Springs, Georgia, when he drew his last breath.

My wife and I were being driven through Beverly Hills many years ago. We passed a home owned by Mickey Rooney. Our driver said, with an air of authority, "That's where JFK shacked up with Marilyn Monroe." Fact or fiction? Who knows? But, the president was known to be something of a womanizer.

California's Governor Arnold Schwartzenager, impregnated his household maid while he was in office

John Edwards, while campaigning for the presidency of the United States, turned his back on his brilliant, devoted lawyer wife who was dying of cancer, and impregnated his mistress.

General David Petraeus, with a PhD. from Princeton, the highest-profile general from our wars in Iraq and Afghanistan, bedded down with his female biographer, Paula Broadwell. Broadwell was distinguished in her own right: two master's degrees, an Olympic-distance triathlete, deputy director of the center on counterterrorism at Tufts University, and a research associate at Harvard.

The reports of their affair reflected the miserable double-standard applied to such events. By many, Petraeus was portrayed as the victim. Broadwell was portrayed as a "stalker," a "home-wrecker," a "temptress;" "his "mistress" (a word for which there is no male counterpart).

Later Patraeus, as head of the CIA, was charged with mishandling government information and was forced to pay a $100,000 fine.

A few years ago the gubernatorial race in Louisiana pitted a Republican Congressman named Vitter, who had been linked to a District of Columbia prostitution ring, against a gentleman named Edwards (no relation to John), whose campaign slogan was, "I won't embarrass you." In the Louisiana of that day Democrats didn't stand a ghost of a chance, but Edwards won 56% of the vote.

And Bill Clinton? It was said of him: "He's a hard dog to keep on the porch."

Long years before the Clinton era, Grover Cleveland, who would later become our nation's president, fathered a child out of wedlock with one Martha Halpin. She had also "slept with" Cleveland's law partner, Oscar Folsom. Uncertain about the paternity, Martha named the child "Oscar Folsom Cleveland."

This chapter has been titled, "our cussedness," because most of us have been weighed and found wanting. As Jesus once said, "Let him who is without sin cast the first stone." Some years ago your author wrote a personal memoir he called,

Feet of Clay on Solid Ground. If we are honest, most of us have feet of clay.

Bless those of you reading these words who have seldom yielded to temptation. And there are those among you, the plain folks these words are written for, who have led circumspect and honorable lives. Again – bless you!

Even so, "cussedness" is a near-universal reality. Most of us can identify with the internal tugs-of-war suggested by these words:

> Within my earthly temple there's a crowd;
> There's one of us that's humble, one that's proud.
> There's one that's broken hearted for his sins.
> There's one that's unrepentant, sits and grins;
> There's one that loves his neighbor as himself,
> And one that cares for naught but fame and pelf.
> From most corroding care should I be free
> If I could once determine which is me.

In all probability they are both me. They are both you and me. If we are normal most if not all of us have been plagued by inner stress and struggle.

This chapter is something of a downer. It details misbehavior, decay, corruption, irrational violence, inner rot, and just plain ugliness; our "cussedness" if you please.

The political realism of both Hans Morgenthau and Reinhold Niebuhr began with the supposition that human nature is flawed. As we read these words most of us acknowledge that we are not everything we should be. We look in a mirror and realize that we are mixed bags; individuals who are far from finished products. But there is more to us than meets the eye. Beyond political realism there is pragmatic idealism.

OUR PROMISE

As indicated – beyond political realism there is pragmatic idealism. While confessing our "cussedness" we must insist that unique promise is also wrapped up in the human story. That promise has been realized in hosts of flesh and blood human beings.

While writing about politics it seems prudent to single out particular political leaders who have personified our promise. We will describe three of them: Vaclav Havel, Aung San Suu Kyi, and Nelson Mandela.

Vaclav Havel, a Czech playwright, dissident and political philosopher, stood center stage during Czechoslovakia's Velvet Revolution in 1989. The communists had imprisoned him. When the non-violent revolution freed him from his prison cell he became the voice of that revolution. He was elected Czechoslovakia's first president and later, the first president of the Czech Republic.

Havel refused his Nobel Peace Prize nomination in 1991, insisting, instead, that it should be given Aung San Suu Kyi. She would say that Havel gave her "a flame of hope," during her darkest days in Burma (Myanmar). Imprisoned by the Russian communists time and time again, Havel did receive the Presidential Medal of Freedom and the Gandhi Peace Prize.

He was known and praised for his anti-consumerism, humanitarianism, environmentalism, political activism, and commitment to a peoples' democracy. He represented the promise of a better tomorrow.

Aung San Suu Kyi was the daughter of General Aung, Burma's (Myanmar's) independence hero, who was assassinated in 1947. She had lived in India, the United Kingdom, Japan, Bhutan and the United States, but returned to Burma in 1988, to care for her ailing mother.

Influenced by Mohatma Gandhi and Martin Luther King, Jr., Suu Kyi was committed to non-violent resistance. Her country was suffering under the cruel heel of its dictator, General Ne Win. She said, "I could not, as my father's daughter, remain indifferent to all what was going on." She traveled across her country pleading for democratic reforms and free elections.

Elections were held in May, 1990. She had been placed under house arrest (she spent 15 years under house arrest), but her National League for Democracy party won convincingly. That made no difference. The military government ignored the results of the election and retained its hold on power. In 1991, Suu Kyi was awarded the Nobel Peace Prize (while under house arrest). In 1995, she made the following statement:

"I have always believed that the future stability and happiness of our nation depends entirely on the readiness of all parties to work for reconciliation. During the years that I have spent under house arrest many parts of the world have undergone almost unbelievable change, and all changes for the better were brought about through dialogue...Once bitter enemies in South Africa are working together for the betterment of their people. Why can't we look forward to a similar process? We have to choose between dialogue and devastation."

Things began to change in Myanmar, in no small measure because of the influence of Aung San Suu Kyi. The military regime relaxed its hold on the people. At long last free elections were held and Suu Kyi's party was allowed to seek office. In 2011, her party won 44 of 45 contested seats in the federal parliament. She said, "We will bring democracy."

Her party controlled the government. Because of a Constitutional technicality Suu Kyi was not permitted to be president. Htin Kyaw was elected president. He named Suu Kyi his foreign minister. Later, a new post was created, and she was named the First and incumbent State Counsellor, and Leader of the National League for Democracy. She may not have been president, but she was definitely in charge.

Francis Sejested, committee chairman of the National League for Democracy, has called Suu Kyi "an outstanding example of the power of powerlessness." Like Havel she represents the promise of a better tomorrow.

And, Nelson Mandela? Many would insist that he was the world's foremost statesman of the 20th century. An attorney, he spent his early years opposing the apartheid policies of the South African government. Charged with sabotage and the attempted overthrow of his government, he was imprisoned for 27 years (he had been given a life sentence). Yielding to international pressure the government released him in 1991. During the latter years of his imprisonment he was assigned to more comfortable quarters and was consulted by government officials for counsel and advice.

In April of 1994, he and President F.W. de Klerk arranged for the first multi-racial election in South Africa's history. A candidate for the presidency, Mandela won a landslide victory and served as president from 1994 to 1999.

His philosophy of life was courageous, humanitarian and inclusive. Many of his words are worth remembering:

"I've learned that courage was not the absence of fear but the triumph over it. The brave man is not he who does not feel afraid, but he who conquers that fear."

"Education is the most powerful weapon which you can use to change the world."

"To be free is not merely to cast off one's chains, but to live in a way that respects and enhances the freedom of others."

"I have fought against white-domination. I have fought against black-domination. I have cherished the ideals of a democratic and free society in which all persons live together in harmony and with equal opportunities. It is an ideal which I hope to live for and achieve. But if need be, it is an ideal for which I am prepared to die."

When Mandela stepped down from the presidency he founded the Nelson Mandela Foundation, a foundation designed to combat poverty and the HIV/AIDS virus in South Africa. The flame of his pragmatic idealism never flickered.

In 1993, Nelson Mandela and President de Klerk were awarded jointly the Nobel Peace Prize for the peaceful termination of apartheid in South Africa. Nelson Mandela, as much as any public servant in the 20th century, represented and symbolized the promise of the human family. While the Morgenthaus, Niebuhrs, and Freuds of this world took a dim view of human nature, there were those like Havel, Suu Kyi and Mandela who personified the hope and promise of the human family.

Carl Rogers was one of the most influential psychologists of the 20th century. Writing about the "world of tomorrow" being shaped by "the person of tomorrow," he described that person. He or she….

- would be open, open to new ways of seeing, new ways of being, new ideas and concepts;
- would desire authenticity, not be two-faced and hypocritical, but real;
- would be skeptical regarding science and technology – life can't be reduced to quantitative measurements – we are persons with minds and spirits;

- would desire wholeness, "with thought, feeling, physical energy, psychic energy, healing energy all being integrated into experience;"
- would wish for intimacy, for new forms of communication, verbal as well as non-verbal, feelingful as well as intellectual;
- would be a process person. willing to take risks; vitally alive in the face of change;
- would be caring, gentle and non-judgmental;
- would have a positive attitude toward nature, seeking to conserve its beauty and energy rather than exploit its resources;
- would be anti-institutional, believing that institutions exist for people, and not the reverse;
- would find their authority within, making their own moral judgments;
- would recognize the unimportance of material things – this is a "toughy", but we tarnish our selfhood if money and material status symbols become our goals;
- and finally, yearning for the spiritual…they would recognize the power and beauty reflected in the lives of Mohatma Gandhi, Mother Teresa, Martin Luther King, Jr., and other humanitarian activists… they would long to experience the harmony of the universe; to become self-transcendent…. People like these would change the direction of human history.

Think of the promise wrapped up in those cited aspirations!

But, we don't have to go to the writings and examples of others. Think of a mother holding and looking down into the face of a new-born baby. That's promise. Think of a parent viewing the graduation of an honor-award winning son. That's promise. Think of a temp employee being promoted to a permanent position. That's promise. Think of a young attorney being asked to become a partner in a law firm. That's promise Or a bench-warmer on a baseball team being upped to the first string – or a lovely young woman being named a beauty queen – or an apprentice carpenter becoming a journeyman – or a cancer patient being given a clean bill of health – or a vigorous, idealistic young merchant being asked to run for public office. You name your own set of hopeful circumstance - there is doubtless promise involved. –

Remember – we are writing about politics for plain folks. But, in the plainest of plain folks, people like you and me, there is promise.

WHERE DOES RELIGION FIT IN – OR DOES IT?

Our frontier settlers were a blend of gun-slinging, heavy drinking, brawling cowpokes and land-grabbers on the one hand, and, at the other end of the spectrum, pioneering and venturesome religious believers.

The Pilgrims, who wanted the faithful to separate from the Church of England, and the Puritans, who wanted to "purify" the Church of England, came to our shores in the early part of the 17th century.

The Church of England had sent 22 clergy to Virginia, the largest and most influential of our colonies, by 1624. They were sent to "evangelize" the colonists.

Quakers, who had been persecuted and imprisoned in 17th century England (by 1650, 10,000 had been imprisoned and nearly 250 had died because of torture and mistreatment), fled to our shores. By 1685, some 8000 of them had sought refuge and new life in Pennsylvania.

Catholics, inspired by Lord Baltimore, had come to what is now the state of Maryland.

Many Jews had settled in port cities along the Atlantic coastline where they could pursue their business interests.

The Catholic Church planted missions in California and Louisiana (primarily in New Orleans) in the 18th and early 19th centuries.

The so-called First Great Awakening (1734-1758) sought to awaken lethargic church members; those who were already identified with organized religion. The prime movers were the Congregationalist Jonathan Edwards, who is best remembered for his sermon, "Sinners in the Hands of an Angry God," and George Whitefield, the portly, cross-eyed son of an English tavern keeper.

A product of and spokesman for the Wesleyan Revival that was jarring the foundations of the Church of England, Whitefield came to the American colonies and founded an orphanage in Georgia. He preached up and down the Atlantic seaboard. No voice of his time did more to bind the colonies together. It is said that if Whitefield had condemned slavery in his messages the history of our land might read quite differently.

Benjamin Franklin heard Whitefield preach in Philadelphia. Tremendously impressed (though never converted to his brand of faith), Franklin befriended and promoted him. Franklin's *Gazette*, the most widely read paper in the colonies, reprinted Whitefield's sermons and devoted 45 issues to his activities. To suggest that Whitefield influenced his moment of time is an understatement.

When the American Revolution unfolded, many churches were Tory in their sympathies. Others justified the Revolution on the basis of their understanding of biblical "truth."

Today there are persuasive televangelists and ill-informed politicians, who insist that we should return to our "Christian origins." They don't know what they are talking about. Our forefathers, men like George Washington, Benjamin Franklin and Thomas Jefferson, were not traditional churchmen; they were Deists. They believed in a push-button God who had gotten things started and then left it up to his "children" to shape events.

John Adams once wrote, "It will never be pretended that the men who set up the American government had interviews with the gods or were in any degree under the inspiration of Heaven."

Our peace treaty with Tripoli (a Muslim state), adopted unanimously by the U.S. Senate in 1797, said, "The government is not in any sense founded on the Christian religion – no pretense arising from religion shall ever produce an interruption of the harmony existing between countries."

Supreme Court Justice William O. Douglas would declare in one of his opinions: "Our institutions presuppose a Supreme Being." True - but our nation's Constitution states explicitly:

"Congress shall make no laws respecting the establishment of religion or prohibiting the free exercise thereof."

When George Herbert Walker Bush argued that no "atheist" should be permitted to hold public office in our country he was refuting his own Constitution.

Thomas Jefferson, in a letter to a Baptist church in New England, spoke of the "wall of separation (between church and state)." Freedom of religion is one of the sacred treasures of our history. Supreme Court justices like Rehnquist and Scalia have disagreed, but that doesn't change the fact – there *is* a "wall of separation."

There was a Second Great Awakening (1800-1840) that sought to reach non-believers; the un-churched. Its most influential spokesman was Charles Finney, a highly educated man and the founder of Oberlin College in Ohio. He is considered the father of modern revivalism.

He believed in applying the Gospel to society and applied the "social gospel" to the abolition of slavery (Tom Paine, an atheist, had called for abolition during our nation's revolution and Benjamin Franklin had founded our nation's first anti-slavery organization in Pennsylvania).

Moravians and Quaker were abolitionists.

In addition to abolition, Finney was committed to temperance and to women's rights. The American Temperance Society was organized in 1826, and within twelve years it boasted 8000 local units and claimed 1½ million members.

And women's rights? From the time of Abigail Adams, our second president's wife; through Harriet Tubman (who will soon be featured on our $20. bills) and Sojourner Truth, escaped slaves who greased the rails of the "underground railway," helping hundreds of slaves escape from their bondage; to Susan B. Anthony, a feminist before "feminism" became a movement; to Margaret Sanger, a birth control advocate when birth control was considered a criminal offense, and who founded of Planned Parenthood – it was *women* who valiantly paved the way for their own "emancipation." Finney was a supportive ally.

Many of the things highlighted by the Second Great Awakening made their way into the laws of the land.

This is not designed to be a detailed text book as we speak of "politics for plain folks," but there are particular matters that need to be remembered as ingredient parts of our story.

As we consider the role of religion in our nation's life there are two fields we will explore in some detail: the place of the Catholic Church in our national psyche, and the role of religion in the civil rights movement.

As we indicated in our consideration of Manifest Destiny, our traditional self-concept was dominated by the ethos of arrogance reflected in our WASP-ish predisposition. Anti-Catholicism had been a negative presence in our country from the beginning. As masses of immigrants poured into the United States from central and southern Europe it became a chronic disease. Samuel Gompers, head of the

American Federation of Labor in the latter part of the 19th century, was vigorously anti-Catholic.

Anti-Catholicism figured prominently in the presidential election of 1928, when Al Smith, a Catholic, was nominated for the presidency by the Democrats. His Catholicism was held against him as he was soundly trounced by Herbert Hoover.

The next Catholic to run for the presidency was John F. Kennedy. Anticipating strands of anti-Catholic thought in the land, he met with a large group of Protestant clergy in Houston, Texas, assuring them that he would not be bound by the rulings of the Vatican. Rather, he would be bound by the U.S. Constitution. He was elected president of the United States. Later Joe Biden, a Catholic, would be our Vice-President.

Religion proved to be a key factor in the civil rights movement. Jesse Jackson, Martin Luther King, Jr., Ralph Abernathy, and Andrew Young were Protestant clergymen. The Southern Christian Leadership Conference was unapologetically anchored in "the faith." Black churches in the South became laboratories where southern blacks were taught methods of passive resistance and non-violent protest; how to be kicked and not kick back; how to be manhandled and not attempt to retaliate – not easy lessons for a proud and brutalized people.

President Lyndon B. Johnson's civil rights, voting rights, and fair housing legislation (initially proposed by John F. Kennedy before his assassination) would never have passed muster had it not been for the persuasive pressures and demands of African American churches and their leaders.

Relate religion's role in politics to recent American presidential primaries and elections. They have featured Mitt Romney, a Mormon "bishop" (in the LDS, a bishop is the same as a "pastor" in most of our churches); Mike Huckabee, a former Arkansas governor and Southern Baptist preacher; and Sarah Palin, a Fundamentalist Christian and one-time vice-presidential candidate who believes in creationism and had a laying-on-of-hands ceremony in Alaska before pursuing her candidacy.

George W. Bush had a 40th birthday party in Colorado Springs. Both his marriage and his business were in trouble. There he had a "heart-warming experience," and is jokingly said to have declared, "Good-bye Jack Daniels/Hello Jesus." He returned to Texas, united with his wife Laura's church, and joined a Bible study and prayer group.

Jimmie Carter speaks unapologetically about his "born again" credentials. Even now, at 90+ years-of-age, he teaches a Sunday school class in his Plains, Georgia church.

Ted Cruz, an ardent Southern Baptist, whose father is a fire-breathing Fundamentalist preacher who has called President Obama a communist (never to be refuted by his son), relied heavily on the "religious vote" during the 2016 primary elections.

Hillary Clinton, influenced in her teens by the Youth Minister of her north Chicago church, embraced the "social gospel" of Jesus and speaks unselfconsciously about her faith and its application to the problems of society. For many years she was part of a prayer group that met regularly in our nation's capitol.

The question is asked – where does religion fit in? To reply succinctly – it fits in all over the place.

Where does religion fit in for you and yours? You will have to answer for yourselves. Do you go to the church? If you do what does it mean to you – if anything? Has your belief system changed over the years? If so, how and why?

What did you learn from your parents – if anything? What about the faith of your family members? What about your neighbors and friends? What about those who determine the direction of your community's life and those who frame public policy? What about your congressmen and governor, or others who impact your lives?

An informed, intelligent religious faith can add an important dimension to their lives - and to yours. As John Danforth argues in his important book, *The Relevance of Religion*, we need to be reminded that: (1) there is realm of spiritual reality beyond the world of our political convictions that helps us give shape to them; and, (2) that beyond the sphere of our think alike, react alike, political cronies and allies, there are hosts of others, equally human, equally thoughtful, who hold political views quite different than our own.

We have been thinking about the various roles of governing bodies, of Manifest Destiny, of the pros and cons of human nature, and about our altered ties with Cuba. We have been thinking about the origins of our "laws and order." In each and every instance religious beliefs, or their absence, have made a difference.

POLITICS WHERE YOU LIVE

You may live in a small town or a large city. You may live on a farm, in a plush suburb, or in a grubby urban slum. No matter – you are subject to decisions your local politicians make.

All communities are affected by civil servants and those employed by your tax dollars: by city managers, mayors, city commissioners and council members; by trash and garbage collectors; by those who provide electricity, utilities, and a wide variety of other things. We tend to take these services for granted, but people working behind the scenes shape our services and comforts or their denial.

In preparing for this chapter your author interviewed a circuit court judge, the mayor of a relatively small city, and a woman who has served two terms on her city council. Without exception they were down-to-earth, intelligent, conscientious, well-intentioned public servants.

The judge had been on the bench for thirty-two years. He was heartened when he was shifted from a criminal court to a court dealing with family matters. He discovered that people under oath "flat-out lied." He avoided going to judges' gatherings "because of the clash of egos." He had become convinced that compromise was an essential ingredient in the formation of policies. He decried the polarization of partisan politics today. He was grateful for the opportunity to be a public servant. He was a good person.

The woman, who served her community as a two-term city council member, took pride in and thoroughly enjoyed her role in community life. She seemed to relish the telephone calls she received from people needing specific services, and was delighted with the fact that those services could be provided (tho' acknowledging that there were a few people who, no matter what you did for them, complained). She spoke of her diligent efforts to get "ordinary citizens" involved in community affairs. She was a good person.

The mayor spoke of his efforts to meet the long neglected needs of the black people of the city and to give them a voice in its governance. He had played a role in rebuilding his community's library, in renovating a city park, and in the development of a golf course. Confessing that the city charter did not give him the authority many other mayors have, he did have the power to make appointments and through that process had been in a position to impact the climate and well-being of his city. He was a good person.

Earlier chapters have spoken of the importance of voting and of the legitimate role of government. It was the ordinary citizens, the "plain folks," who had made possible by the votes they had cast, all of the things the judge, the council-woman, and the mayor, had been able to accomplish. Elections had put them in office.

We have been considering "politics for plain folks." Plain folks have far more muscle than they sometimes realize.

A new minister had come to town. He met with a judge (not the one interviewed for this chapter) for breakfast. She (this time the judge was a woman) was a member of his congregation and asked him what he hoped to accomplish while serving the people. His answers seemed mundane. She pressed him. "But what of *real significance* do you want to see happen?"

About 4000 African Americans lived on the west side of their city; literally "on the other side of the tracks." During the early years of their city's life the blacks had been politically disenfranchised and had been neglected or ignored. The church the preacher and the judge were related to was an affluent and influential community of faith. They decided they would get the church involved.

A "blue ribbon committee" was named to give specific consideration to making some significant changes. A "west side story" equal to anything Broadway has produced was forthcoming. The mayor, a school board official, a land developer, representatives of social service agencies, a retired minister with extensive experience in urban renewal in Florida's Dade County, and a few other concerned members, as well as a couple of eager young people, were appointed to serve.

The group determined not to provide "answers" from outside the community, but simply to listen and wait for a sense of direction. Hearings were held and some of them were wild. Angry, conflicting voices made their demands. The group met with a land developer who was gobbling up choice west side properties for his mercenary gain. It met with merchants, law enforcement officers, real estate operators, and others who needed to be involved.

Lake Island Park was an expanse of neglected land wedged between black residents and commercial developments on a major thoroughfare The blue ribbon committee was asked by the mayor to redesign and refurbish the park. Rather than presuming to speak *for* the west side the committee set up an organization with co-chairs, one white and one African American, for each of its working committees. After long months of hearty endeavor the park was renovated and restored.

Working with the city commission and park officials it planned and "manned" (most of the co-chairs were women) a day-long celebration in October of 1996. The Methodist bishop in Florida, Cornelius Henderson, the first African American episcopal leader to be assigned to Florida by his church, was the featured speaker.

The highlight of the day was the ribbon cutting ceremony dedicating a bridge that had been installed in the park. It was called Unity Bridge. The mayor and the bishop wielded the scissors.

One of the co-chairs of the event, a member of the sponsoring church, spoke. He said, "You can't build and keep and grow a bridge called Unity without the effort of the whole community. That's hard work, but it's worth it. Unity is a bridge worth building."

An organization called Bridgebuilders was formed. It became an umbrella organization that led, in 2000, to the formation of an independent 501(c)(3) entity, a Neighborhood Development Corporation. It was a corporation designed to encourage and facilitate housing and development activities. It recruited volunteers to engage in neighborhood cleanup and landscaping efforts.

Bridgebuilders met each month in a black Baptist church involving citizens from both sides of the tracks (white citizens of the city lived on the east of railroad tracks that split the city down the middle; blacks in the city lived on the west side). The Bridgebuilders' charter insisted that one of its missions was to "ensure that all persons living in (their city) work together to create racial harmony and secure neighborhoods, and make a sensitive and informed response to the needs of the residents."

An interesting side-bar: Bridgebuilders, ably assisted by civic clubs, sponsored an Easter sunrise service every year. It featured community choirs and salt-and-pepper children choirs, with both Catholic and Protestant clergy presiding. A symbol of Unity!

Why go to these lengths to describe events in one community? Because we are writing about "politics for plain folks." Ordinary citizens, plain folks, were responsible for the decision-making and constructive activities that led to the literal rebirth of a major part of a city.

Your author and his wife used to attend a church in which the pastor ended each sermon by asking, "What about you? What about you? What about you." Sometimes I felt like responding, "So what? So what? So what?" But, the question is on target. *What about you?*

This chapter is titled: "The Politics Where You Live." You who are reading these words live in a variety of locations. Who are its titular heads? Who are those decision-makers and actors who really get things done? They are often not the same.

Consider your own community, and, in the quietness of the moment, answer a series of questions:

- Are the policy makers in your community serving the basic needs of you and others like you?
- Do they feather their own nests while ignoring the well-being of people like you and others like you?
- Do outside interests (corporations not based in your community or politicians who seem committed to ideals and interests far removed from you and your compatriots) maintain control over your well-being?
- Who have you voted for – and why? As we have considered the role of government and the power of the ballot box, we have insisted that people like us, plain folks, shape our own destinies. Who among your neighbors and friends, or those in

your community who you trust, have run for public office? Have you encouraged them to do so? If not, why not?

- Have you identified the enemies of "the general welfare" where you live? The sources of racial bigotry? The economic interests that subvert the health of community life? The indifference and apathy that seem to paralyze so much community life?

- Are you yourself a bridge-builder? As a candidate for the U.S. presidency reminded us many years ago, we should be building bridges, not walls.

We are approaching the end of our time together. We have covered a lot of territory. Let me end with a radical reminder. You – yes, *you* – can be a vital participant in shaping the health and welfare of your surroundings. Don't betray your singular opportunity in this moment of time. Don't be a part of the problem because of your indifference or your refusal to act. Be an integral part of the solution, embracing each and every opportunity you have to make ours a healthier, more just and righteous society.

Who knows – you might even run for office yourself.

Printed in the United States
By Bookmasters